A CELEBRATION OF LIFE

WHEN A LOVED ONE DIES

Redemptorist Communications

W: www.redcoms.org
E: sales@redcoms.org
T: 00353 (0)1 4922 488

Published by:
Redemptorist Communications
Tel: 00353 (0)1 492 2488
www.redcoms.org
sales@redcoms.org

....

Copyright © 2015 Redemptorist Communications
1st Edition 1999
2nd Edition 2006
3rd Edition 2010
Text: Gerard Moloney, C.Ss.R. & George Wadding, C.Ss.R.
Design: Tanika Design

....

With ecclesiastical permission
+Diarmuid,
Archbishop of Dublin
Given at Dublin this 11th day of February 2015

....

Scripture extracts taken from the Jerusalem Bible, published and copyright 1966, 1967 and 1968 by Darton Longman & Todd Ltd. and Doubleday & Co. Inc., used by permission of the publishers; extracts from The Psalms: A New Translation, published by Harper Collins Ltd., reproduced by permission of A. P Watt Ltd. on behalf of the Grail, England.

....

Thanks to Fanagans Funeral Directors for advice on the role of the Funeral Director.

....

CONTENTS

INTRODUCTION

The death of a loved one can be one of the most traumatic experiences of our lives. Our world is turned upside down. We are plunged into sadness and grief, and yet there are so many arrangements to be made, so many things to do. It can be so hard to cope.

This book will be a help. It offers practical advice on what to do when a loved one dies.

- It explains the role of the priest and of the Funeral Director.

- It takes you through the funeral liturgy, and helps you to plan it.

- It contains a wide selection of readings and psalms for use during the funeral Mass.

- It offers reflections on bereavement and how it affects us, including a detailed look at the grieving process.

- It describes the Christian understanding of death, and deals in a straightforward way with many questions people ask about death and how the Church understands it.

- It provides scripture reflections for personal use that will soothe and comfort.

- At the back of the book, there are some useful addresses of groups and organisations that can offer help.

Use this book in whatever way you wish. Our hope and prayer is that it will provide you with some practical help and encouragement during these difficult days.

"Do not let your hearts be troubled.
Trust in God still, and trust in me.
There are many rooms in my Father's house;
if there were not I should have told you.
I am going now to prepare a place for you,
and after I have gone and prepared you a place,
I shall return to take you with me;
so that where I am you may be too."
....

(John 14:1-3)

IN GOD'S LOVING HANDS

The death of someone you love is always traumatic. You may have been waiting for your loved one to die for weeks or months, expecting it. Yet the actual happening is still stunning. One moment the person you love is alive; the next he or she is dead. Until that moment, there is always the possibility, however remote, that the person will go on living. The moment of death is the moment reality hits home: your loved one is gone. There is no turning the clock back.

SO MUCH TO DO

There is also so much to do. Family and friends have to be contacted, the priest and funeral director informed, arrangements made, tea and hospitality provided as people come to sympathise. There may be some family members you have not seen in a long time, others who have travelled overseas. There are the details of the removal and the funeral Mass to be worked out.

NO TIME TO GRIEVE

In the midst of the busyness, you may not have time yet to begin to grieve. Or you may be carried along in a kind of daze, not feeling the full impact of your loss. But once the funeral is over and things settle back down, the reality of your loss will sink in. You may be overwhelmed with all kinds of feelings: shock, anger, despair, guilt. You may feel lost, alone, isolated. You may even feel that God has abandoned you. You have trusted in God and now your faith seems empty.

DARKEST MOMENTS

But even in your darkest moments, you need not fear, for God is with you. He is close to you. He feels your pain. "Do not let your hearts be troubled," Jesus says. "Trust in God still and trust in me. There are many rooms in my Father's house." This is the wonderful promise of Jesus –that he has prepared a place for those who love him.

So turn to God now. Place all your tears, all your grief, all your anxiety and doubts in his hands. Ask him to take care of your deceased loved one. He will give you the strength and support you need. He will bathe you and your loved one in his all-embracing love.

WHAT TO DO WHEN SOMEONE YOU LOVE DIES

What you must do when someone you love dies will depend on where and in what circumstances the death occurred.

If the death is expected
- Call the doctor who has been attending your loved one. The doctor will issue a medical certificate of the cause of death.
- Call the funeral director.
- Call the priest, if he has not already been in attendance when your loved one passed away.

If the death is unexpected
- Call the doctor who has been attending your loved one. The doctor may issue the medical certificate if he or she is satisfied as to the cause of death and has been in attendance within the previous 28 days.
- Call the funeral director.
- Call the priest.

If, however, the doctor is unable to issue the medical certificate
- Call the police, who will in turn contact the coroner. The coroner will instruct a pathologist to examine the body and report the cause of death to him. If the pathologist's report to the coroner shows that the death was due to natural causes, the coroner will issue the Medical Certificate.

- In the case of death by accident, or in suspicious circumstances, there will be a post-mortem examination. If the cause of death is still unclear, the coroner may call for an inquest.

- The funeral director cannot remove the body or proceed with the funeral arrangements without the knowledge that the medical certificate will be issued.

CREMATION

if the death is expected
- If the body of your loved one is to be cremated, the deceased's doctor must have attended within 28 days before the death, and must first view the body after death and fill out a special form before the funeral director can proceed with the arrangements.

if the death is unexpected
- The coroner will arrange with the funeral director the necessary medical documentation for the crematorium authority.

THE ROLE OF THE FUNERAL DIRECTOR

After the death of a loved one, there are many decisions that will have to be made. The funeral director will be able to assist you with the detailed planning of the funeral so that you can concentrate on family and friends and on comforting one another. The funeral director will co-ordinate the funeral arrangements, including:

- Assistance in the selection and style of the coffin.
- Preparation and dressing of the body.
- Provision of hearse, bearers and transportation for the removal to the funeral home, the church and the cemetery.

- Grave opening (and purchase of a new grave if required).
- The following disbursements will be arranged: church offerings, gratuities, soloist, organist, flowers.
- All cremation arrangements.
- Newspaper obituary notice.

The funeral director will also attend to any special requests for which the deceased may have left instructions. (Note: it is important to know your loved one's wishes. If you do not already know them, it may be necessary to read the will to find out.)

THE ROLE OF THE PRIEST

Your priest will be there to support and help you in any way he can during the difficult days around the death of your loved one. The priest has three principal roles: as minister of comfort, teacher of faith, and presider at the funeral liturgies.

He will, if at all possible, visit before the death to administer the last rites, to pray with the dying person and the family, and to provide comfort, consolation and hope.

He will visit after the death to accompany the family in their grief, to pray with them for the deceased, to listen and sympathise and to answer any questions they may have.

He will also discuss the details of the funeral liturgy. He will help in the selection of readings, prayer of the faithful, appropriate hymns and music. If you do not feel up to planning the details of the liturgy yourself, your priest will be happy to do it for you. He may also want to know some details about the life and personality of the deceased that will help him in preparing the funeral homily.

During this time and in the days and weeks after the funeral, he will be there to help you through the stages of grief and to provide you with the emotional and faith support you need.

"We want you to be quite certain about those who have died, to make sure that you do not grieve about them, like the other people who have no hope. We believe that Jesus died and rose again, and that it will be the same for those who have died in Jesus: God will bring them with him."

(1Thessalonians. 4:13)

PLANNING YOUR LOVED ONE'S FUNERAL LITURGY

The Church encourages you to be as fully involved as you can in planning your loved one's funeral liturgy. It is the final journey of your loved one.

In the liturgy, we celebrate the life of faith of your loved one; we commend him or her to the Lord, we support and pray for all those who mourn, and we seek strength in the promise of the Lord that he will not forget his own. In planning the liturgy, you will need to:

- Provide your priest with some biographical information about your deceased loved one that will help him in preparing the funeral homily.

- Select the readings for the funeral Mass. Depending on the circumstances, you may decide to have either one or two readings before the gospel reading. You will find a large selection of suitable readings in this booklet. But you are free to choose others. Should you decide to have two readings before the gospel, it is preferable to have a different reader for each.

- Select the responsorial psalm, which comes between the first and second readings. You will find a number of responsorial psalms in this booklet, but, again, you are free to choose others. In making your choice, you should take into account the Church's recommendation that, if at all possible, the responsorial psalm or the response to it should be sung.

- Choose or compose the general intercessions, for the Prayer of the Faithful, which come after the homily. In the general intercessions we pray not only for the deceased and his or her family and friends but also for all the dead and those who mourn them, as well as for the needs of the wider community. You will find a selection of general intercessions in this booklet. One or more family members or friends should read the general intercessions.

- Choose family members or friends of the deceased to bring the gifts of bread and wine to the altar. You should keep in mind, though, that the presentation of the gifts is not the time to carry up personal memorabilia or symbols of the life of the deceased. The best time for this is at the reception of the body.

- Choose the hymns and music for the funeral Mass. The hymns should be selected from those regularly sung during Sunday Mass, and should express our strong belief in the resurrection, which is the basis of Christian hope. They should not include favourite secular songs or music of the deceased not appropriate for a funeral liturgy.

"But Christ has in fact been raised from the dead, the first-fruits of all who have fallen asleep. Death came through one man and in the same way the resurrection of the dead has come through one man. Just as all people die in Adam so all will be brought to life in Christ."

(1 Corinthians 15:20–22)

CELEBRATING THE FUNERAL

Your priest will provide you with whatever advice or help you need in planning the liturgy.

The funeral has three principal stages or moments: the vigil and reception of the body at the church; the central funeral liturgy, which normally includes Mass; and the rite of committal. These ritual moments together form your loved one's final journey of farewell. They celebrate our faith in Christ's resurrection and his consoling presence with us at this time.

THE WAKE AND VIGIL FOR THE DECEASED

There has been a long tradition in Ireland of having a wake for the deceased. It is a time when the family and friends of the deceased "stay awake" to mourn the passing of the loved one, to share memories of his or her life, to accept the sympathy and support of the Christian community, and to pray that the deceased may have eternal life. The wake normally takes place in the home of the deceased or in a funeral home. There are a number of prayer services that can take place during the wake, and which may be led by a priest, deacon or lay person, including the rosary. The wake normally ends with "The Vigil for the Deceased." The Vigil is similar to the Liturgy of the Word at Sunday Mass, and is composed of the introductory rite, readings and psalm, some prayers of intercession, and a concluding rite.

RECEPTION OF THE BODY AT THE CHURCH

The rite of reception of the body at the church may take place on the evening before the funeral Mass or on the morning of the funeral itself. This ceremony has great significance because the church is the place where the community of faith gathers for worship, and where the deceased also worshipped. It is the place where people enter into new life through baptism and participation in the Eucharist. It is now the place where the community gathers to greet the deceased as one of their own.

The rite of reception of the body begins by sprinkling it with holy water at the church door, the procession into the church, and opening prayer. The readings and a brief homily follow. Their purpose is to proclaim our hope in the resurrection and to offer support to those who mourn. The service ends with the prayers of intercession, Our Father, and a concluding prayer.

USE OF CHRISTIAN SYMBOLS

Some important symbols are used during the funeral liturgies.

The Paschal Candle is placed close to the coffin when it is received at the church. It reminds us of Christ's presence among us and of his victory over death, a victory in which we share through our baptism.

Holy Water is used to sprinkle the coffin when it is received at the church, and during the final commendation at the end of the funeral Mass. It may also be used on other occasions during the wake and funeral: at the gathering in the presence of the body, during the vigil service, when the coffin is being closed, and at the time of committal or burial. The holy water reminds us of our baptism and the baptism of our deceased loved one.

A Pall may be placed on the coffin by family members or friends when it is received at the church. The pall is a large white cloth that covers the coffin during the liturgy. It is a reminder of the white robe that is put on the newly baptised to symbolise his or her new life in Christ. It is also a reminder that all are equal in the eyes of God.

A Bible or Cross may be placed on the coffin. The Bible reminds us that Christians are called to live by the Word of God, and that it is by being faithful to that word that we gain eternal life.

The cross reminds us that Christians are marked by the sign of the cross in baptism, and that it was through his suffering on the cross that Jesus won for us the promise of resurrection.

Incense is used to honour the body of the deceased, who through baptism became a living temple of God's presence. It is also a sign of the community's prayers for the deceased rising up to heaven, and a sign of farewell.

THE FUNERAL MASS AND FINAL COMMENDATION

The funeral Mass is the central liturgical celebration for the deceased. It is similar in structure to the Sunday Mass. You will already have chosen the readings and general intercessions. If at all possible, you should also ensure that there is singing and music.

After communion, there is the final commendation. It is the beginning of our final farewell to our deceased loved one.

The focus is on separation, on letting go. But the focus is also on hope, as we look forward to the promise of eternal life. The priest goes to a place near the coffin. He invites us to pray in silence for our deceased loved one whom we now entrust to the merciful embrace of God. The coffin is then sprinkled with holy water and incensed. This may be done during or after the song of farewell. The song of farewell is a high point of this rite. It expresses our hope that Christ will take our deceased loved one to himself, and that we will one day be reunited in the heavenly kingdom. The rite finishes with the prayer of commendation. The final part of the journey now begins. A hymn should be sung as the body of the deceased is carried from the church.

THE COMMITTAL

The body is taken to its final resting place. There we take our leave of our deceased loved one. The rite of committal is simple: the priest leads a short scripture reading, and blesses the grave. There is a prayer of committal, during which the coffin is lowered into the grave, some intercessions, the Our Father, and finally, a concluding prayer over the people. The grave and coffin may be blessed with holy water. Some earth may also be scattered on the coffin. After the concluding prayer, a decade of the Rosary may be said.

CREMATION

If the body of your deceased loved one is to be cremated, the rite of committal takes place at the crematorium. Prayers from the rite of committal and other texts may be said if the ashes are to be interred at some time after the cremation.

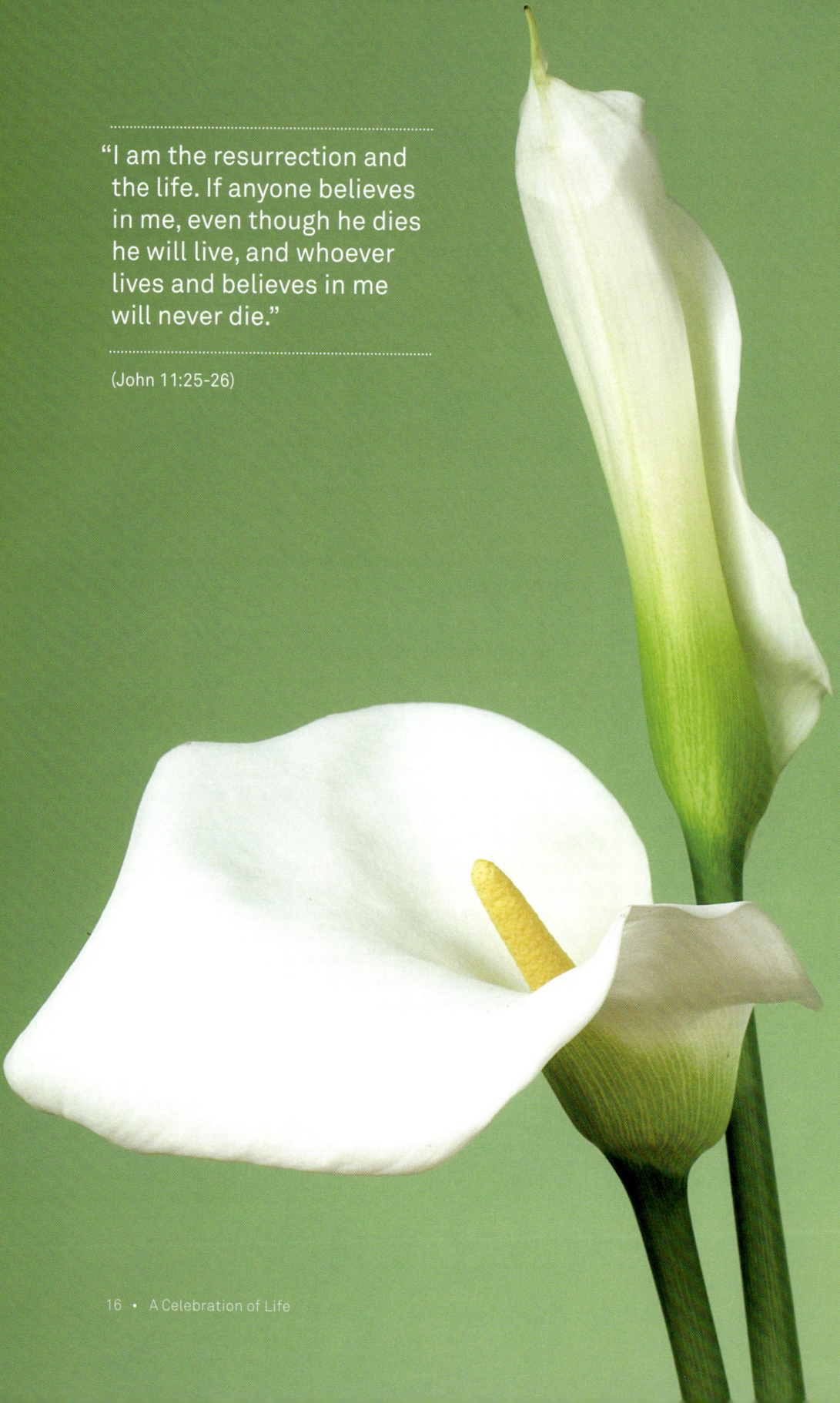

"I am the resurrection and the life. If anyone believes in me, even though he dies he will live, and whoever lives and believes in me will never die."

(John 11:25-26)

CHOOSING THE READINGS

The readings are a central part of your loved one's funeral Mass. You may choose one Old Testament and/or one New Testament reading before the Gospel reading. The Responsorial Psalm comes after the first reading.

The following is a helpful guide but you are free to choose readings from scripture and a psalm other than those contained in this booklet. Your priest will help guide you on the choice of readings.

The location of each reading and psalm in the Lectionary is noted below. The Lectionary is the official book of readings used at Mass.

FIRST READINGS

A. FROM THE OLD TESTAMENT

FIRST READING 1
(LECTIONARY OLD TESTAMENT 1)

A reading from the book of Job [19:1.23–27]
Job said: 'Ah, would that these words of mine were written down,
inscribed on some monument
with iron chisel and engraving tool,
cut into the rock for ever.
This I know: that my Avenger lives,
and he, the Last, will take his stand on earth.
After my awaking, he will set me close to him,
and from my flesh I shall look on God.
He whom I shall see will take my part:
these eyes will gaze on him and find him not aloof.'

The word of the Lord.

FIRST READING 2
(LECTIONARY OLD TESTAMENT 2B)

A reading from the book of Wisdom [3:1-6.9]
The souls of the virtuous are in the hands of God,
no torment shall ever touch them.
In the eyes of the unwise, they did appear to die,
their going looked like a disaster,
their leaving us, like annihilation;
but they are in peace.
If they experienced punishment as men see it,
their hope was rich with immortality;
slight was their affliction, great will their blessing be.
God has put them to the test
and proved them worthy to be with him;
he has tested them like gold in a furnace,
and accepted them as a holocaust.
They who trust in him will understand the truth,
those who are faithful will live with him in love;
for grace and mercy await those he has chosen.

The word of the Lord.

FIRST READING 3
(LECTIONARY OLD TESTAMENT 3)

A reading from the book of Wisdom [4:7–15]
The virtuous man, though he died before his time, will find rest.
Length of days is not what makes age honourable,
nor number of years the true measure of life;
understanding, this is a person's grey hairs,
untarnished life, this is ripe old age.
He has sought to please God, so God has loved him;
as he was living among sinners, he has been taken up.
He has been carried off so that evil may not warp his understanding
or treachery seduce his soul;
for the fascination of evil throws good things into the shade,

and the whirlwind of desire corrupts a simple heart.
Coming to perfection in so short a while, he achieved
long life;
his soul being pleasing to the Lord,
he has taken him quickly from the wickedness around him.
Yet people look on, uncomprehending;
it does not enter their heads
that grace and mercy await the chosen of the Lord,
and protection, his holy ones.

The word of the Lord.

FIRST READING 4
(LECTIONARY OLD TESTAMENT 4)

A reading from the prophet Isaiah [25:6-9]
On this mountain,
the Lord of hosts will prepare for all peoples
a banquet of rich food.
On this mountain he will remove
the mourning veil covering all peoples,
and the shroud enwrapping all nations,
he will destroy Death for ever.
The Lord will wipe away
the tears from every cheek;
he will take away his people's shame
everywhere on earth,
for the Lord has said so.
That day, it will be said: See, this is our God
in whom we hoped for salvation;
the Lord is the one in whom we hoped.
We exult and we rejoice
that he has saved us.

The word of the Lord.

FIRST READING 5
(LECTIONARY OLD TESTAMENT 5)

A reading from the book of Lamentations [3:17-26]
My soul is shut out from peace;
I have forgotten happiness.
And now I say, 'My strength is gone,
that hope which came from the Lord'.
Brooding on my anguish and affliction
is gall and wormwood.
My spirit ponders it continually
and sinks within me.
This is what I shall tell my heart,
and so recover hope:

the favours of the Lord are not all past,
his kindnesses are not exhausted;
every morning they are renewed;
great is his faithfulness.
'My portion is the Lord' says my soul
'and so I will hope in him.'
The Lord is good to those who trust him,
to the soul that searches for him.
It is good to wait in silence
for the Lord to save.

The word of the Lord.

FIRST READING 6
(LECTIONARY OLD TESTAMENT 7)

A reading from the second book of Maccabees [12:43–45]
Judas, the leader of the Jews, took a collection from the people individually, amounting to nearly two thousand drachmae, and sent it to Jerusalem to have a sacrifice for sin offered, an altogether fine and noble action, in which he took full account of the resurrection. For if he had not expected the fallen to rise again it would have been superfluous and foolish to pray for the dead, whereas if he had in view the splendid recompense reserved for those who make a pious end, the thought was holy and devout. This was why he had this atonement sacrifice offered for the dead, so that they might be released from their sin.

The word of the Lord.

FIRST READING 7 (NOT IN LECTIONARY)

A reading from the Book of Tobit [4: 1-5, 15-17, 20]

Tobit thought: 'I have come to the point of praying for death; I should do well to call my son Tobias and talk to him'. He summoned his son Tobias and told him: 'When I die, give me an honourable burial. Honour your mother, and never abandon her all the days of your life. Do all that she wants, and give her no reason for sorrow. Remember, my child, all the risks she ran for your sake when you were in her womb. And when she dies, bury her at my side in the same grave'.
'My child, be faithful to the Lord all your days. Never entertain the will to sin or to transgress his laws. Do good works all the days of your

life, never follow ways that are not right; for if you act in truthfulness, you will be successful in all your actions, as all men are if they practice what is right...'

'Be careful, my child, in all you do, well-disciplined in all your behaviour. Do to no one what you would not want done to you. Do not drink wine to the point of drunkenness; do not let excess be your travelling companion. Give your bread to those who are hungry, and your clothes to those who are naked. Whatever you own in plenty, devote a proportion to almsgiving; and when you give alms, do not do it grudgingly'... So now, my child, remember these precepts and never let them fade from your heart.'

Tobias then answered his father Tobit, 'Father,' he said, 'I will do everything you have told me.'

The word of the Lord.

B. FROM THE NEW TESTAMENT

FIRST READING 8 (LECTIONARY NEW TESTAMENT FIRST READINGS 2)

A reading from the book of Revelation [14:13]

I, John, heard a voice from heaven say to me, 'Write down: happy are those who die in the Lord! Happy indeed, the Spirit says; now they can rest for ever after their work, since their good deeds go with them.'

The word of the Lord.

FIRST READING 9 (LECTIONARY NEW TESTAMENT FIRST READINGS 3)

A reading from the book of Revelation [20:11-21:1]

I, John, saw a great white throne and the One who was sitting on it. In his presence, earth and sky vanished, leaving no trace. I saw the dead, both great and small, standing in front of his throne, while the book of life was opened, and other books opened which were the record of what they had done in their lives, by which the dead were judged.

The sea gave up all the dead who were in it; Death and Hades were emptied of the dead that were in them; and every one was judged according to the way in which he had lived. Then Death and Hades were thrown into the burning lake. This burning lake is the second death; and anybody whose name could not be found written in the book of life was thrown into the burning lake.

Then I saw a new heaven and a new earth; the first heaven and the first earth had disappeared now, and there was no longer any sea.

The word of the Lord.

FIRST READING 10 (LECTIONARY NEW TESTAMENT FIRST READINGS 4)

A reading from the book of Revelation [21:1–7]

I, John, saw a new heaven and a new earth; the first heaven and the first earth had disappeared now, and there was no longer any sea. I saw the holy city, and the new Jerusalem, coming down from God out of heaven, as beautiful as a bride all dressed for her husband. Then I heard a loud voice call from the throne, 'You see the city? Here God lives among men. He will make his home among them: they shall be his people, and he will be their God; his name is God-with-them. He will wipe away all tears from their eyes; there will be no more death, and no more mourning or sadness. The world of the past has gone.'

Then the One sitting on the throne spoke: 'Now I am making the whole of creation new,' he said. 'I will give water from the well of life free to anybody who is thirsty; it is the rightful inheritance of the one who proves victorious, and I will be his God and he a son to me.'

The word of the Lord.

RESPONSORIAL PSALMS

RESPONSORIAL PSALM 1 [PSALM 26]
(LECTIONARY AFTER OLD TESTAMENT FIRST
READING 1)

Response:
The Lord is my light and my help.

The Lord is my light and my help;
whom shall I fear?
The Lord is the stronghold of my life;
before whom shall I shrink? R.

There is one thing I ask of the Lord,
for this I long,
to live in the house of the Lord
all the days of my life,
to savour the sweetness of the Lord,
to behold His temple. R.

O Lord, hear my voice when I call;
have mercy and answer.
It is your face, O Lord, that I seek;
hide not your face. R.

I am sure I shall see the Lord's goodness
in the land of the living.
Hope in him, hold firm and take heart.
Hope in the Lord. R.

RESPONSORIAL PSALM 2 [PSALM 114]
(LECTIONARY AFTER OLD TESTAMENT FIRST
READING 2)

Response:
I will walk in the presence of the Lord,
in the land of the living

How gracious is the Lord and just;
our God has compassion.
The Lord protects the simple hearts;
I was helpless so he saved me. R

I trusted, even when I said:
'I am sorely afflicted',
and when I said in my alarm:
'No one can be trusted'. R

O precious in the eyes of the Lord
is the death of his faithful.
Your servant, Lord, your servant am I;
you have loosened my bonds. R

RESPONSORIAL PSALM 3 [PSALM 22]
(LECTIONARY AFTER OLD TESTAMENT FIRST
READING 4)

Response:
The Lord is my shepherd;
There is nothing I shall want.

The Lord in my shepherd;
there is nothing I shall want.
Fresh and green are the pastures
where he gives me repose.
Near restful waters he leads me,
to revive my drooping spirit. R.

He guides me along the right path;
he is true to his name.
If I should walk in the valley of darkness
no evil would I fear.
You are there with your crook and your staff;
with these you give me comfort. R.

You have prepared a banquet for me
in the sight of my foes.
My head you have anointed with oil;
my cup is overflowing. R.

Surely goodness and kindness shall follow me
all the days of my life.
In the Lord's own house shall I dwell
for ever and ever. R.

RESPONSORIAL PSALM 4 [PSALM 24]
(LECTIONARY AFTER OLD TESTAMENT FIRST
READING 5)

Response:
Those who hope in you, Lord,
shall not be disappointed.

Remember your mercy, Lord,
and the love you have shown from of old.
In your love remember me,
because of your goodness, O Lord. R

Relieve the anguish of my heart
and set me free from my distress.
See my affliction and my toil
and take all my sins away. R
Preserve my life and rescue me.
Do not disappoint me, you are my refuge.

May innocence and uprightness protect me:
for my hope is in you, O Lord. R

RESPONSORIAL PSALM 5 [PSALM 41]
(LECTIONARY AFTER OLD TESTAMENT FIRST READING 6)
Response:
My soul is thirsting for God,
the God of my life.

Like a deer that yearns
for running streams,
so my soul is yearning
for you, my God. R

My soul is thirsting for God,
the God of my life;
when can I enter and see
the face of God? R

These things will I remember
as I pour out my soul:
how I would lead the rejoicing crowd
into the house of God,
amid cries of gladness and thanksgiving,
the throng wild with joy. R

RESPONSORIAL PSALM 6 [PSALM 102]
(LECTIONARY AFTER OLD TESTAMENT FIRST READING 7)
Response:
The Lord is compassion and love.

The Lord is compassion and love,
slow to anger and rich in mercy.
He does not treat us according to our sins
nor repay us according to our faults. R

As a father has compassion on his children,
the Lord has pity of those who fear him;
for he knows of what we are made,
he remembers that we are dust. R

As for man, his days are like grass;
he flowers like the flower of the field;
the wind blows and he is gone
and his place never sees him again. R

But the love of the Lord is everlasting
upon those who fear him;
he justice reaches out to children's children
when they keep his covenant in truth. R

RESPONSORIAL PSALM 7 [PSALM 23]
(NOT IN LECTIONARY)
Response:
The Lord's is the earth and its fullness.

The Lord's is the earth and its fullness,
the world and all its peoples.
It is he who set it on the seas;
on the waters he made it firm. R

Who shall climb the mountain of the Lord?
Who shall stand in his holy place?
Those with clean hands and pure heart,
who desire not worthless things. R

They shall receive blessings from the Lord
and reward from the God who saves them.
Such are the people who seek him,
seek the face of the God of Jacob. R

RESPONSORIAL PSALM 8 [PSALM 83]
(NOT IN LECTIONARY)
Response:
My soul is longing for the courts of the Lord.

The sparrow finds herself a home
and the swallow a nest for her brood;
she lays her young by your altars,
Lord of hosts, my king and my God. R

They are happy, who dwell in your house,
for ever singing your praise.
They are happy, whose strength is in you,
in whose hearts are the roads to Sion. R

As they go through the Bitter Valley
they make it a place of springs.
They walk with ever growing strength,
they will see the God of gods in Sion. R

For the Lord God is a rampart, a shield;
he will give us his favour and glory.
The Lord will not refuse any good
to those who walk without blame. R

RESPONSORIAL PSALM 9 [PSALM 129]
(LECTIONARY AFTER NEW TESTAMENT FIRST
READING 2)

Response:
Out of the depths I cry to you, O Lord. Lord.

Out of the depths I cry to you, O Lord,
Lord, hear my voice.
O let your ears be attentive
to the voice of my pleading. R.

If you, O Lord, should mark our guilt,
Lord, who would survive?

But with you is found forgiveness:
for this we revere you. R.

My soul is waiting for the Lord,
I count on his work.
My soul is longing for the Lord
more than watchman for daybreak. R.

Because with the Lord there is mercy
and fullness of redemption,
Israel indeed he will redeem
from all its iniquity. R.

SECOND READINGS

FROM THE NEW TESTAMENT

SECOND READING 1 (LECTIONARY, FIRST
READING EASTER SEASON 1)

A reading from the Acts of the Apostles
[10:34-43]

Peter addressed Cornelius and his household:
'The truth I have now come to realise,' he said,
'is that God does not have favourites, but that
anybody of any nationality who fears God and
does what is right is acceptable to him.
'It is true, God sent his word to the people of
Israel, and it was to them that the good news
of peace was brought by Jesus Christ – but
Jesus Christ is Lord of all people. You must
have heard about the recent happenings in
Judaea; about Jesus of Nazareth and how
he began in Galilee, after John had been
preaching baptism. God had anointed him
with the Holy Spirit and with power, and
because God was with him, Jesus went about
doing good and curing all who had fallen
into the power of the devil. Now I, and those
with me, can witness to everything he did
throughout the countryside of Judaea and
in Jerusalem itself: and also to the fact that
they killed him by hanging him on a tree, yet
three days afterwards God raised him to
life and allowed him to be seen, not by the
whole people but only by certain witnesses
God had chosen beforehand. Now we are
those witnesses – we have eaten and drunk
with him after his resurrection from the
dead – and he has ordered us to proclaim
this to his people and to tell them that God
has appointed him to judge everyone alive or
dead. It is to him that all the prophets bear
this witness: that all who believe in Jesus will
have their sins forgiven through his name.'

The word of the Lord.

SECOND READING 2
(LECTIONARY NEW TESTAMENT 1)

A reading from the letter of St Paul to the
Romans [5:5-11]

Hope is not deceptive, because the love of
God has been poured into our hearts by
the Holy Spirit which has been given us. We
were still helpless when at his appointed
moment Christ died for sinful men. It is not
easy to die even for a good man – though
of course for someone really worthy, a man
might be prepared to die – but what proves
that God loves us is that Christ died for us
while we were still sinners. Having died to
make us righteous, is it likely that he would
now fail to save us from God's anger? When
we were reconciled to God by the death of
his Son, we were still enemies; now that we
have been reconciled, surely we may count
on being saved by the life of his Son? Not
merely because we have been reconciled but
because we are filled with joyful trust in God,
through our Lord Jesus Christ, through whom
we have already gained our reconciliation.

The word of the Lord.

SECOND READING 3
(LECTIONARY NEW TESTAMENT 2)

A reading from the letter of St Paul to the Romans [5:17-21]

If it is certain that death reigned over everyone as the consequence of one man's fall, it is even more certain that one man, Jesus Christ, will cause everyone to reign in life who receives the free gift that he does not deserve, of being made righteous. Again, as one man's fall brought condemnation on everyone, so that good act of one man brings everyone life and makes them justified. As by one man's disobedience many were made sinners, so by one man's obedience many will be made righteous. When law came, it was to multiply the opportunities of falling, but however great the number of sins committed, grace was even greater; and so, just as sin reigned wherever there was death, so grace will reign to bring eternal life thanks to the righteousness that comes through Jesus Christ our Lord.

The word of the Lord.

SECOND READING 4
(LECTIONARY NEW TESTAMENT 3)

A reading from the letter of St Paul to the Romans [6:3-4, 8-9]

When we were baptised in Christ Jesus we were baptised in his death; in other words, when we were baptised we went into the tomb with him and joined him in death, so that as Christ was raised from the dead by the Father's glory, we too might live a new life. We believe that having died with Christ we shall return to life with him: Christ, as we know, having been raised from the dead will never die again. Death has no power over him any more.

The word of the Lord.

SECOND READING 5
(LECTIONARY NEW TESTAMENT 4)

A reading from the letter of St Paul to the Romans [8:14–23]

Everyone moved by the Spirit is a child of God. The spirit you received is not the spirit of slaves bringing fear into our lives again; it is the spirit of children, and it makes us cry out, 'Abba, Father!' The Spirit himself and our spirit bear united witness that we are children of God. And if we are children we are heirs as well: heirs of God and coheirs with Christ, sharing his sufferings so as to share his glory.

I think that what we suffer in this life can never be compared to the glory, as yet unrevealed, which is waiting for us. The whole creation is eagerly waiting for God to reveal his children. It was not for any fault on the part of creation that it was made unable to attain its purpose, it was made so by God; but creation still retains the hope of being freed, like us, from its slavery to decadence, to enjoy the same freedom and glory as the children of God. From the beginning till now the entire creation, as we know, has been groaning in one great act of giving birth; and not only creation, but all of us who possess the first-fruits of the Spirit, we too groan inwardly as we wait for our bodies to be set free.

The word of the Lord.

SECOND READING 6
(LECTIONARY NEW TESTAMENT 5)

A reading from the letter of St Paul to the Romans [8:31–35. 37–39]

With God on our side who can be against us? Since God did not spare his own Son, but gave him up to benefit us all, we may be certain, after such a gift, that he will not refuse us anything he can give. Could anyone accuse those that God has chosen? When God acquits, could anyone condemn? Could Christ Jesus? No! He not only died for us – he rose from the dead, and there at God's right hand he stands and pleads for us.

Nothing therefore can come between us and the love of Christ, even if we are troubled or worried, or being persecuted, or lacking food or clothes, or being threatened or even attacked. These are the trials through which we triumph, by the power of him who loved us. For I am certain of this: neither death nor life, no angel, no prince, nothing that exists, nothing still to come, not any power, or height or depth, nor any created thing, can ever come between us and the love of God made visible in Christ Jesus our Lord.

The word of the Lord.

SECOND READING 7
(LECTIONARY NEW TESTAMENT 6)

A reading from the letter of St Paul to the Romans [14:7-12]

The life and death of each of us has its influence on others; if we live, we live for the Lord; and if we die, we die for the Lord, so that alive or dead we belong to the Lord. This explains why Christ both died and came to life, it was so that he might be Lord both of the dead and of the living. We shall all have to stand before the judgement seat of God; as scripture says: By my life – it is the Lord who speaks – every knee shall bend before me, and every tongue shall praise God. It is to God, therefore, that each of us must give an account of himself.

The word of the Lord.

SECOND READING 8
(LECTIONARY NEW TESTAMENT 7)

A reading from the first letter of St Paul to the Corinthians [15:20–23]

Christ has been raised from the dead, the first-fruits of all who have fallen asleep. Death came through one man and in the same way the resurrection of the dead has come through one man. Just as all die in Adam, so all will be brought to life in Christ; but all of them in their proper order; Christ as the first-fruits and then, after the coming of Christ, those who belong to him.

The word of the Lord.

SECOND READING 9
(LECTIONARY NEW TESTAMENT 8)

A reading from the first letter of St Paul to the Corinthians [15:51–57]

I will tell you something that has been secret; that we are not all going to die, but we shall all be changed. This will be instantaneous, in the twinkling of an eye, when the last trumpet sounds. It will sound, and the dead will be raised, imperishable, and we shall be changed as well, because our present perishable nature must put on imperishability and this mortal nature must put on immortality.

When this perishable nature has put on imperishability, and when this mortal nature has put on immortality, then the words of scripture will come true: Death is swallowed up in victory. Death, where is your victory? Death, where is your sting? Now the sting of death is sin, and sin gets its power from the Law. So let us thank God for giving us the victory through our Lord Jesus Christ.

The word of the Lord.

SECOND READING 10
(LECTIONARY NEW TESTAMENT 10)

A reading from the second letter of St Paul to the Corinthians [5:1. 6–10]

We know that when the tent that we live in on earth is folded up, there is a house built by God for us, an everlasting home not made by human hands, in the heavens.
We are always full of confidence, then, when we remember that to live in the body means to be exiled from the Lord, going as we do by faith and not by sight – we are full of confidence, I say, and actually want to be exiled from the body and make our home with the Lord. Whether we are living in the body or exiled from it, we are intent on pleasing him. For all the truth about us will be brought out in the law court of Christ, and each of us will get what he deserves for the things he did in the body, good or bad.

The word of the Lord

SECOND READING 11
(LECTIONARY NEW TESTAMENT 11)

A reading from the letter of St Paul to the Philippians [3:20-21]

For us, our homeland is in heaven, and from heaven comes the saviour we are waiting for, the Lord Jesus Christ, and he will transfigure these wretched bodies of ours into copies of his glorious body. He will do that by the same power with which he can subdue the whole universe.

The word of the Lord.

SECOND READING 12
(LECTIONARY NEW TESTAMENT 12)

A reading from the first letter of St Paul to the Thessalonians [4:13–18]

We want you to be quite certain, brothers, about those who have died, to make sure that you do not grieve about them, like the other people who have no hope. We believe that Jesus died and rose again, and that it will be the same for those who have died in Jesus: God will bring them with him. We can tell you this from the Lord's own teaching, that any of us who are left alive until the Lord's coming will not have any advantage over those who have died. At the trumpet of God, the voice of the archangel will call out the command and the Lord himself will come down from heaven; those who have died in Christ will be the first to rise, and then those of us who are still alive will be taken up in the clouds, together with them, to meet the Lord in the air. So we shall stay with the Lord for ever. With such thoughts as these you should comfort one another.

The word of the Lord.

SECOND READING 13
(LECTIONARY NEW TESTAMENT 13)

A reading from the second letter of St Paul to Timothy [2:8-13]

Remember the Good News that I carry, 'Jesus Christ risen from the dead, sprung from the race of David;' it is on account of this that I have my own hardships to bear, even to being chained like a criminal – but they cannot chain up God's news. So I bear it all for the sake of those who are chosen so that in the end they may have the salvation that is in Christ Jesus and the eternal glory that comes with it.
Here is a saying that you can rely on:
If we have died with him, then we shall live with him.
If we hold firm, then we shall reign with him.
If we disown him, then he will disown us.
We may be unfaithful, but he is always faithful,
for he cannot disown his own self.

The word of the Lord.

SECOND READING 14 (NOT IN LECTIONARY)

A reading from the second letter of St Paul to Timothy [4:6-8]

As for me, my life is already being poured away as libation, and the time has come for me to be gone. I have fought the good fight to the end; I have run the race to the finish; I have kept the faith; all there is to come now is the crown of righteousness reserved for me, which the Lord, the righteous judge, will give me on that Day; and not only to me but to all those who have longed for his Appearing.

The word of the Lord.

SECOND READING 15
(LECTIONARY NEW TESTAMENT 14)

A reading from the first letter of St John [3:1–2]

Think of the love that the Father has lavished on us,
by letting us be called God's children;
and that is what we are.
Because the world refused to acknowledge him,
therefore it does not acknowledge us.
My dear people, we are already the children of God
but what we are to be in the future has not yet been revealed;
all we know is, that when it is revealed we shall be like him
because we shall see him as he really is.

The word of the Lord.

SECOND READING 16
(LECTIONARY NEW TESTAMENT 15)

A reading from the first letter of St John [3:14-16]

We have passed out of death and into life, and of this we can be sure because we love one another.
If you refuse to love, you must remain dead;
to hate your brother is to be a murderer, and murderers, as you know, do not have eternal life in them.
This has taught us love –
that he gave up his life for us;
and we, too, ought to give up our lives for our brothers and sisters.

The word of the Lord.

SECOND READING 17 (NOT IN LECTIONARY)

A reading from the first letter of St John [4:7-12.17]

My dear people,
let us love one another
since love comes from God
and everyone who loves is begotten by God
and know God.
Anyone who fails to love can never have
known God,
because God is love.
God's love for us was revealed
when God sent into the world his only Son
so that we could have life through him;
this is the love I mean;
not our love for God,
but God's love for us when he sent his Son
to be the sacrifice that takes our sins away.
My dear people,
since God has loved us so much,
we too should love one another.
No one has ever seen God;
but as long as we love one another.
No one has ever seen God;
but will live in us
and his love will be complete in us.
Love will come to its perfection in us
when we can face the day of Judgement
without fear.

The word of the Lord.

GOSPEL READINGS

GOSPEL READING 1
(LECTIONARY GOSPEL 1)

A reading from the holy Gospel according to Matthew [5:1–12]

Seeing the crowds, Jesus went up the hill.
There he sat down and was joined by his
disciples. Then he began to speak. This is
what he taught them:
'How happy are the poor in spirit;
theirs is the kingdom of heaven.
Happy the gentle:
they shall have the earth for their heritage.
Happy those who mourn;
they shall be comforted.
Happy those who hunger and thirst for what
is right:
they shall be satisfied.
Happy the merciful:
they shall have mercy shown them.
Happy the pure in heart:
they shall see God.
Happy the peacemakers:
they shall be called children of God.
Happy those who are persecuted in the cause
of right:
theirs is the kingdom of heaven.
'Happy are you when people abuse you and
persecute you and speak all kinds of calumny
against you on my account. Rejoice and be
glad, for your reward will be great in heaven.'

The Gospel of the Lord.

GOSPEL READING 2
(LECTIONARY GOSPEL 2)

A reading from the holy Gospel according to Matthew [11:25-30]

Jesus exclaimed, 'I bless you, Father, Lord of
heaven and of earth, for hiding these things
from the learned and the clever and revealing
them to mere children. Yes, Father, for that
is what it pleased you to do. Everything has
been entrusted to me by my Father; and no
one knows the Son except the Father, just as
no one knows the Father except the Son and
those to whom the Son chooses to reveal him.
'Come to me, all you who labour and are
overburdened, and I will give you rest.
Shoulder my yoke and learn from me, for I am
gentle and humble in heart, and you will find
rest for your souls. Yes, my yoke is easy and
my burden light.'

The Gospel of the Lord.

GOSPEL READING 3
(LECTIONARY GOSPEL 3)

A reading from the holy Gospel according to Matthew [25:1-13]

Jesus spoke this parable to his disciples:
'The kingdom of heaven will be like this: Ten
bridesmaids took their lamps and went to
meet the bridegroom. Five of them were
foolish and five were sensible: the foolish
ones did take their lamps, but they brought

no oil, whereas the sensible ones took flasks of oil as well as their lamps. The bridegroom was late and they all grew drowsy and fell asleep. But at midnight there was a cry. "The bridegroom is here! Go out and meet him." At this, all those bridesmaids woke up and trimmed their lamps, and the foolish ones said to the sensible ones, "Give us some of your oil: our lamps are going out." But they replied, "There may not be enough for us and for you; you had better go to those who sell it and buy some for yourselves." They had gone off to buy it when the bridegroom arrived. Those who were ready went in with him to the wedding hall and the door was closed. The other bridesmaids arrived later. "Lord, Lord," they said, "open the door for us." But he replied, "I tell you solemnly, I do not know you." So stay awake, because you do not know either the day or the hour.'

The Gospel of the Lord.

GOSPEL READING 4 (LECTIONARY GOSPEL 4)

A reading from the holy Gospel according to Matthew[25:31–40]

Jesus said to his disciples; 'When the Son of Man comes in his glory, escorted by all the angels, then he will take his seat on his throne of glory. All the nations will be assembled before him and he will separate men one from another as the shepherd separates sheep from goats. He will place the sheep on his right hand and the goats on his left. Then the King will say to those on his right hand, "Come, you whom my Father has blessed, take for your heritage the kingdom prepared for you since the foundation of the world. For I was hungry and you gave me food; I was thirsty and you gave me drink; I was a stranger and you made me welcome; naked and you clothed me, sick and you visited me, in prison and you came to see me." Then the virtuous will say to him in reply, "Lord, when did we see you hungry and feed you; or thirsty and give you drink? When did we see you a stranger and make you welcome; naked and clothe you; sick or in prison and go to see you?" And the King will answer, "I tell you solemnly, in so far as you did this to one of the least of these brothers of mine, you did it to me."

The Gospel of the Lord.

GOSPEL READING 5 (LECTIONARY GOSPEL 5)

A reading from the holy Gospel according to Mark [15:33–39]

When the sixth hour came there was darkness over the whole land until the ninth hour. And at the ninth hour Jesus cried out in a loud voice, 'Eloi, Eloi, lama sabachthani?' which means, 'My God, my God, why have you deserted me?' When some of those who stood by heard this, they said, 'Listen, he is calling on Elijah.' Someone ran and soaked a sponge in vinegar and, putting it on a reed, gave it to him to drink saying, 'Wait and see if Elijah will come to take him down.' But Jesus gave a loud cry and breathed his last. And the veil of the Temple was torn in two from top to bottom. The centurion, who was standing in front of him, had seen how he had died and he said, 'In truth this man was a son of God.'

The Gospel of the Lord.

GOSPEL READING 6 (LECTIONARY GOSPEL 6)

A reading from the holy Gospel according to Luke [7:11–17]

Jesus went to a town called Nain, accompanied by his disciples and a great number of people. When he was near the gate of the town it happened that a dead man was being carried out for burial, the only son of his mother, and she was a widow. And a considerable number of the townspeople were with her. When the Lord saw her he felt sorry for her. 'Do not cry,' he said. Then he went up and put his hand on the bier and the bearers stood still, and he said, 'Young man, I tell you to get up'. And the dead man sat up and began to talk, and Jesus gave him to his mother. Everyone was filled with awe and praised God saying, 'A great prophet has appeared among us; God has visited his people'. And this opinion of him spread throughout Judaea and all over the countryside.

The Gospel of the Lord.

GOSPEL READING 7
(LECTIONARY GOSPEL 7)

A reading from the holy Gospel according to Luke [12:35–40]

Jesus said to his disciples: 'See that you are dressed for action and have your lamps lit. Be like men waiting for their master to return from the wedding feast, ready to open the door as soon as he comes and knocks. Happy those servants whom the master finds awake when he comes. I tell you solemnly, he will put on an apron, sit them down at table and wait on them. It may be in the second watch he comes, or in the third, but happy those servants if he finds them ready. You may be quite sure of this, that if the householder had known at what hour the burglar would come, he would not have let anyone break through the wall of his house. You too must stand ready, because the Son of Man is coming at an hour you do not expect.'

The Gospel of the Lord.

GOSPEL READING 8
(LECTIONARY GOSPEL 8)

A reading from the holy Gospel according to Luke [23:33.39-43]

When the soldiers reached the place called The Skull, they crucified Jesus there and the two criminals also, one on the right, the other on the left.
One of the criminals hanging there abused him. 'Are you not the Christ?' he said. 'Save yourself and us as well.' But the other spoke up and rebuked him. 'Have you no fear of God at all?' he said. 'You got the same sentence as he did, but in our case we deserved it: we are paying for what we did. But this man has done nothing wrong. Jesus,' he said, 'remember me when you come into your kingdom.' 'Indeed, I promise you,' he replied, 'today you will be with me in paradise.'

The Gospel of the Lord.

GOSPEL READING 9
(LECTIONARY GOSPEL 9)

A reading from the holy Gospel according to Luke [23:44–46. 50. 52–53. 24:1–6]

It was about the sixth hour and, with the sun eclipsed, a darkness came over the whole land until the ninth hour. The veil of the Temple was torn right down the middle; and when Jesus had cried out in a loud voice, he said, 'Father, into your hands I commit my spirit'. With these words he breathed his last. Then a member of the council arrived, an upright and virtuous man named Joseph. This man went to Pilate and asked for the body of Jesus. He then took it down, wrapped it in a shroud and put him in a tomb which was hewn in stone in which no one had yet been laid.
On the first day of the week, at the first sign of dawn, the women went to the tomb with the spices they had prepared. They found that the stone had been rolled away from the tomb, but on entering discovered that the body of the Lord Jesus was not there. As they stood there not knowing what to think, two men in brilliant clothes suddenly appeared at their side. Terrified, the women lowered their eyes. But the two men said to them, 'Why look among the dead for someone who is alive? He is not here, he has risen.'

The Gospel of the Lord.

GOSPEL READING 10
(LECTIONARY GOSPEL 10)

A reading from the holy Gospel according to Luke [24:13–16. 28-35]

On the first day of the week, two of the disciples were on their way to a village called Emmaus, seven miles from Jerusalem, and they were talking together about all that had happened. Now as they talked this over, Jesus himself came up and walked by their side; but something prevented them from recognising him.
When they drew near to the village to which they were going, he made as if to go on; but they pressed him to stay with them. 'It is nearly evening,' they said, 'and the day is almost over.' So he went in to stay with them. Now while he was with them at table, he took the bread and said the blessing; then he broke it and handed it to them. And their eyes were opened and they recognised him; but he had vanished from their sight. Then they said to each other, 'Did not our hearts burn within us as he talked to us on the road and explained the scriptures to us?'

They set out that instant and returned to Jerusalem. There they found the Eleven assembled together with their companions, who said to them, 'Yes, it is true. The Lord has risen and has appeared to Simon.' Then they told their story of what had happened on the road and how they had recognised him at the breaking of bread.

The Gospel of the Lord.

GOSPEL READING 11
(LECTIONARY GOSPEL 11)

A reading from the holy Gospel according to John [5:24-29]

Jesus said to the Jews:
'I tell you most solemnly,
whoever listens to my words,
and believes in the one who sent me,
has eternal life;
without being brought to judgement
he has passed from death to life.
I tell you most solemnly,
the hour will come – in fact it is here already
– when the dead will hear the voice of the Son of God,
and all who hear it will live.
For the Father, who is the source of life,
has made the Son the source of life;
and, because he is the Son of Man,
has appointed him supreme judge.
Do not be surprised at this,
for the hour is coming
when the dead will leave their graves
at the sound of his voice;
those who did good
will rise again to life;
and those who did evil, to condemnation.
I can do nothing by myself;
I can only judge as I am told to judge,
and my judging is just,
because my aim is to do not my own will,
but the will of him who sent me.'

The Gospel of the Lord.

GOSPEL READING 12
(LECTIONARY GOSPEL 12)

A reading from the holy Gospel according to John [6:37-40]

Jesus said to the crowd:
'All that the Father gives me will come to me,
and whoever comes to me
I shall not turn him away;
Because I have come from heaven
not to do my own will,
but to do the will of the one who sent me.
Now the will of him who sent me
is that I should lose nothing
of all that he has given to me,
and that I should raise it up on the last day.
Yes, it is my Father's will
that whoever sees the Son and believes in him
shall have eternal life,
and that I shall raise him up on the last day.'

The Gospel of the Lord.

GOSPEL READING 13
(LECTIONARY GOSPEL 13)

A reading from the hold Gospel according to John [6:51–58]

Jesus said to the crowd:
'I am the living bread which has come down from heaven.
Anyone who eats this bread will live for ever;
and the bread that I shall give
is my flesh, for the life of the world.'
Then the Jews started arguing with one another: 'How can this man give us his flesh to eat?' they said. Jesus replied:
'I tell you most solemnly,
if you do not
eat the flesh of the Son of Man
and drink his blood,
you will not have life in you.
Anyone who does eat my flesh and drink my blood
has eternal life,
and I shall raise him up on the last day.
For my flesh is real food
and my blood is real drink.
He who eats my flesh and drinks my blood
lives in me
and I live in him.
As I, who am sent by the living Father,
myself draw life from the Father,
so whoever eats me will draw life from me.
This is the bread come down from heaven;
not like the bread our ancestors ate:
they are dead,
but anyone who eats this bread will live for ever.'

The Gospel of the Lord.

GOSPEL READING 14
(LECTIONARY GOSPEL 14)

A reading from the holy Gospel according to John [11:17–21]

On arriving at Bethany, Jesus found that Lazarus had been in the tomb for four days already. Bethany is only about two miles from Jerusalem, and many Jews had come to Martha and Mary to sympathise with them over their brother. When Martha heard that Jesus had come she went to meet him. Mary remained sitting in the house. Martha said to Jesus, 'If you had been here, my brother would not have died, but I know that, even now, whatever you ask of God, he will grant you.' 'Your brother,' said Jesus to her, 'will rise again.' Martha said, 'I know he will rise again at the resurrection on the last day'. Jesus said:
'I am the resurrection and the life.
If anyone believes in me, even though he dies he will live,
and whoever lives and believes in me will never die.
Do you believe this?'
'Yes, Lord,' she said, 'I believe that you are the Christ, the Son of God, the one who was to come into this world.'

The Gospel of the Lord.

GOSPEL READING 15
(LECTIONARY GOSPEL 15)

A reading from the holy Gospel according to John [11:32–45]

Mary the sister of Lazarus went to Jesus, and as soon as she saw him she threw herself at his feet, saying, 'Lord, if you had been here, my brother would not have died.' At the sight of her tears, and those of the Jews who followed her, Jesus said in great distress, with a sigh that came straight from the heart, 'Where have you put him?' They said, 'Lord, come and see.' Jesus wept; and the Jews said, 'See how much he loved him!' But there were some who remarked, 'He opened the eyes of the blind man, could he not have prevented this man's death?' Still sighing, Jesus reached the tomb: it was a cave with a stone to close the opening. Jesus said, 'Take the stone away.' Martha said to him, 'Lord, by now he will smell; this is the fourth day." Jesus replied,

'Have I not told you that if you believe you will see the glory of God?' So they took away the stone. Then Jesus lifted up his eyes and said:
'Father, I thank you for hearing my prayer.
I know indeed that you always hear me, but I speak
for the sake of all these who stand round me, so that they may believe it was you who sent me.'
When he had said this, he cried in a loud voice, 'Lazarus, here! Come out!' The dead man came out, his feet and hands bound with bands of stuff and a cloth round his face. Jesus said to them, 'Unbind him, let him go free.'
Many of the Jews who had come to visit Mary and had seen what he did believed in him.

The Gospel of the Lord.

GOSPEL READING 16
(LECTIONARY GOSPEL 16)

A reading from the holy Gospel according to John [12:23-26]

Jesus said to his disciples:
'Now the hour has come
for the Son of Man to be glorified.
I tell you, most solemnly,
unless a wheat grain falls on the ground and dies,
it remains only a single grain;
but if it dies,
it yields a rich harvest.
Anyone who loves his life loses it;
anyone who hates his life in this world
will keep it for the eternal life.
If a man serves me, he must follow me,
wherever I am, my servant will be there too.
If anyone serves me, my Father will honour him.'

The Gospel of the Lord.

GOSPEL READING 17
(LECTIONARY GOSPEL 17)

A reading from the holy Gospel according to John [14:1–6]

Jesus said to his disciples:
'Do not let your hearts be troubled.
Trust in God still, and trust in me.
There are many rooms in my Father's house;
if there were not, I should have told you.

I am going now to prepare a place for you,
and after I have gone and prepared you a place,
I shall return to take you with me;
so that where I am
you may be too.
You know the way to the place where I am going.
Thomas said, 'Lord, we do not know where you are going, so how can we know the way?'
Jesus said:
'I am the Way, the Truth and the Life.
No one can come to the Father except through me.'

The Gospel of the Lord.

GOSPEL READING 18
(LECTIONARY GOSPEL 18)

A reading from the holy Gospel according to John [17:24-26]

Jesus raised his eyes to heaven and said:
'Father,
I want those you have given me
to be with me where I am,
so that they may always see the glory
you have given me
because you loved me
before the foundation of the world.
Father, Righteous One,
the world has not known you,
but I have known you,
and these have known
that you have sent me.
I have made your name known to them
and will continue to make it known
so that the love with which you loved me may be in them,
and so that I may be in them.'

The Gospel of the Lord.

GOSPEL READING 19
(LECTIONARY GOSPEL 19)

A reading from the holy Gospel according to John [19:17-18.25-30]

Carrying his own cross, Jesus went out of the city to the place of the skull or, as it was called in Hebrew, Golgotha, where they crucified him with two others, one on either side with Jesus in the middle.
Near the cross of Jesus stood his mother and his mother's sister, Mary the wife of Clopas, and Mary of Magdala. Seeing his mother and the disciple he loved standing near her, Jesus said to his mother, 'Woman this is your son.' Then to the disciple he said, 'This is your mother.'
After this, Jesus knew that everything had now been completed, and to fulfil the scripture perfectly he said:
'I am thirsty.'
A jar of vinegar stood there, so putting a sponge soaked in the vinegar on a hyssop stick they held it up to his mouth. After Jesus had taken the vinegar he said, 'It is accomplished;' and bowing his head he gave up his spirit.
It was Preparation Day, and to prevent the bodies remaining on the cross during sabbath – since that sabbath was a day of special solemnity – the Jews asked Pilate to have the legs broken and the bodies taken away. Consequently the soldiers came and broke the legs of the first man who had been crucified with him and then of the other. When they came to Jesus, they found he was already dead, and so instead of breaking his legs one of the soldiers pierced his side with a lance; and immediately there came out blood and water. This is the evidence of one who saw it – trustworthy evidence, and he knows he speaks the truth – and he gives it so that you may believe as well. Because all this happened to fulfil the words of scripture: Not one bone of his will be broken; and again, in another place scripture says: They will look on the one whom they have pierced.
After this, Joseph of Arimathaea, who was a disciple of Jesus – though a secret one because he was afraid of the Jews – asked Pilate to let him remove the body of Jesus. Pilate gave permission, so they came and took it away. Nicodemus came as well – the same one who had first come to Jesus at night-time – and he brought a mixture of myrrh and aloes, weighing about a hundred pounds.

The Gospel of the Lord.

SUGGESTED GENERAL INTERCESSIONS

The general intercessions come after the homily. In the general intercessions we pray for the deceased and his or her family and friends, for all the dead and those who mourn them, and for the needs of the wider community. Some or all of those given here may be used, or new intercessions may be composed.

Priest:
God our Father has given us victory over sin and death through his Son, Jesus Christ. Let us turn to him in our hour of need, and pray to him with confidence.

Response:
Lord, graciously hear us.

Reader:
In baptism N. was given the pledge of eternal life. May he/she now be admitted to the company of the saints.

Lord, hear us.

Reader:
For N.: that Christ may have mercy on his/her soul, and grant him/her full pardon for his/her sins.

Lord, hear us.

Reader:
For the family of N.: that in these difficult and dark days they may be sustained by their faith, and by the knowledge that they will be reunited with N. one day in God's heavenly kingdom.

Lord, hear us.

Reader:
For our deceased relatives and friends: that God may bring them into the light of his presence, and give them a share in his glory.

Lord, hear us.

Reader:
For all the faithful departed: that they may see God face to face in the kingdom of heaven.

Lord, hear us.

Reader:
For all here present: that our remembrance of N. may be a source of comfort and strength to us.

Lord, hear us.

Reader:
For the gift of life, which we all share and is very precious: may the Lord help us to be more aware of the gifts and talents given to us, particularly those we so often take for granted and may we use them to make the world a better place.

Lord, hear us.

Reader:
The gift of life, which we all share, is very precious. Lord, make us more aware of the gifts and talents that you have given us, particularly those that we so often take for granted. May we use them to make the world a better place.

Lord, hear us.

Reader:
For all of us gathered here: that we may remember at all times, but especially at times of trouble and anxiety, that we are loved by God and that he will take care of us.

Lord, hear us.

(Relevant prayer for death after an illness)

Reader:
We pray for all nurses and carers, particularly the nurses and carers who were so good to N. in the last months of his/her life.

Lord, hear us

Priest:
Father, into your hands we commend the soul of our brother/sister, N. Look gently upon him/her, and bring him/her home to your kingdom where death will be no more. We ask this through Christ our Lord.